JB
SEARCHES
Beyond the
Big Cities

Finding Employment
in Medium to Small-Sized Markets

J⬤B
SEARCHES
Beyond the
Big Cities

Inquiza Communications

Sarah Fuller

Published by Inquiza Communications, L.L.C., P.O. Box 306, West Monroe, Louisiana 71294
http://www.inquiza.com

Printed and bound in the United States of America.

Library of Congress Control Number: 2008920801
ISBN-13: 978-0-9800595-0-2

Editing: Rachel Knox and Gayle Bogart
Cover Design: Stephanie D. Walker

Disclaimer
The information in this book should not be construed as legal, financial, or other such advice. You should consult a licensed professional for the above advice. The publisher and author have made their best efforts to ensure the accuracy of the information in this book and make no warranties and accept no responsibility for damages, real or perceived, related to its use.

CONTENTS

PREFACE

I wrote this handbook for job searching in medium to small-sized cities out of pure frustration with the job resources that were available when I began my own search in a small city. The majority of job advice books that I found focused on career searches with a big city perspective: send out targeted resumes to many businesses in your area (The yellow pages in my town lists fifty businesses, not fifty tons). Find numerous job leads in your town using large Internet job search sites. (Heck, the closest these job sites get to my town are the first two letters!)

Whether you are one of the many people who move from metropolitan to smaller areas each year, or a long time resident of a medium to small-sized city, this job search book is for you. It is specifically designed with the non-big city dweller in mind. This book offers realistic advice about searching for a job or career position outside of the major cities.

The information that you will find in this book is based on my personal, friends, and coworkers' experiences, as well as, lots of research on the latest in online and offline job resources. I have been in both the job hunter and employer role in a variety of smaller job markets. I have drawn upon the knowledge that I have acquired through those positions to provide you with the job search strategies and resources that you will find in this book.

I think you will find the information very helpful in your job search.

INTRODUCTION

Some Job Hunting Elbow Room

Whether you live where you do out of preference, necessity, a spouse's job, or myriad other reasons, non-major metropolitan living has its pluses.

Enjoy the Commute or Lack Thereof

The average commute time in the United States, according to a Bureau of Transportation Statistics' survey[1], is just over 26 minutes. Another survey[2] shows that in large cities such as New York (38.3 minutes), Chicago (33.2 minutes), Philadelphia (29.4 minutes), and Los Angeles (29 minutes), commute time exceeds that average time. These statistics should not lead you to believe that medium to small-sized cities are free of all traffic problems. I figure, though, that living where you do not have traffic helicopters buzzing overhead and 24 hour traffic alert radio stations gives you a better chance for smoother driving.

A House Price That Keeps You From Having to Mortgage Your Pets and Children

In many cases, housing prices and the cost of living are lower in less populated areas. Have you noticed how people move out to suburban areas in search of lower housing costs? How about the big city job transplants who are pleasantly surprised that they get so much more house for the money just outside of big city commuting range.

Ah! Smell the Country Air

Get out of the big city and smell the fresh country air. Don't commercials, movies, and books often romanticize escape from life in the frenetic metropolis? Even detergent makers are getting into the act with scents designed to evoke visions of the bucolic countryside when you wear those freshly washed jeans.

Although not every small place is a "bed of fresh smelling roses," less populated areas may have an advantage in general. According to the "State of the Air: 2007" report by the American Lung Association[3], some of the country's largest cities/metro regions can be found among the list of most polluted by short-term particulates. It makes logical sense that more people means more output in many cases. Of the 26 cities with the cleanest air record regarding short-term particulate pollution, only 6 had populations over 400,000 persons.

Less Crowd, Less Crime (Generally)

As with pollution, more people concentrated in an area often leads to more crime. According to the Bureau of Justice Statistics[4], almost one-quarter of U.S. homicides occur in cities with populations greater than a million. Additionally, large cities are more commonly the locations of drug and gang-related killings.

A Sense of Connectedness

The smaller the size of the city where individuals live, the more connected, in one way or another, they find themselves with other residents. One reason is that paths tend to cross with others more often because there are less people to interact with and fewer businesses to patronize. I remember when I was a child growing up in a small city, it seemed like Mom would always run into about five people she knew at the grocery store every time we shopped. (That made for some long and dreaded shopping trips, but I digress.)

CHAPTER ONE

Network to Work

The *interconnectedness of people's lives* in smaller markets is a key factor in determining how to approach the job search. Because there is such a concentration on person-to-person interaction and a value placed on "being in the know" about other people, networking clearly stands out as the number one job search tool.

The largest part of the job search effort should be focused on networking, with online and print resources serving to enhance this effort. This mix is what will garner the most job offers for the largest number of people in medium to small-sized markets in the least amount of time.

Okay, I feel your shudders of horror. Most of us would much rather scrub the kitchen floor until it shines like a diamond than pick up the phone and call somebody that we don't know to discuss job opportunities. I think the universal fear of rejection takes over.

I am here to tell you as a member of the "phone networking phobics anonymous" club, once you get going, things get easier and the fear of widespread rejection begins to dissipate. In my experience, not one person has ever yelled at me for asking for his or her employment advice.

Look at it this way. What is networking really? It is asking for advice to help you access the right people who may be able to hire you for a great position. Along the way you get to know some nice individuals.

Where to Start Your Search

I suggest that you head to the nearest table to get your job search off to a jump-start. Grab a chair and make a list of people you know and who you think that these people might know. If you listed your family and believe that you are stuck, try thinking about some of the categories of people below to build your list.

- Friends and neighbors
- Members of your church, synagogue, mosque, or other religious organizations
- Parents and teachers at your child's school
- Members of any clubs or sports teams in which you or your children are involved
- Past co-workers, bosses, or clients

Networking Contacts to Take You to the Next Level

To further expand your networking list, consider adding the following contacts:

Local Chambers of Commerce

Chambers of Commerce are essentially networks of businesses, often organized regionally. The Chambers represent their membership to their communities as well as in wide geographic areas.

A variety of Chambers of Commerce exist and many post their member lists online or have print membership directories available. Some libraries keep copies of up-to-date directories in their reference sections.

Chambers are also great places to volunteer your time. They can generally use the free assistance, and you get the benefit of meeting lots of influential individuals! The following are some of the major Chambers of Commerce:

U.S. Chamber of Commerce
http://www.uschamber.com/
This federation represents more than three million businesses and organizations. Within the U.S. Chamber's site is a directory that will lead you to a Chamber near you.

National Black Chamber of Commerce
http://www.nationalbcc.org/
The National Black Chamber of Commerce reaches 100,000 black owned businesses. The website offers links to black chambers in various parts of the United States through its resource section.

United States Hispanic Chamber of Commerce
http://www.ushcc.com/
This organization serves the Hispanic business community with more than 150 affiliated Hispanic Chambers of Commerce. Check out the "Locate a Chamber" feature prominently displayed on the home page as well as the "Business Hotlinks" section under the Resources tab.

Minority Chamber of Commerce

http://www.minoritychamber.net/

This organization is focused on helping businesses with a minimum of 51 percent minority ownership. The Minority Chamber of Commerce is based in South Florida, but offers resources that may be of assistance nationally.

Other Chamber of Commerce resource links include

Chamber of Commerce.com

http://www.chamberofcommerce.com/

This site offers a search directory for Chambers of Commerce, Better Business Bureaus, and Convention and Visitors Bureaus under the "Resource Directory" section.

Chamber of Commerce, USA Directory

http://www.2chambers.com/

Similar to the site above, you can find listings for Chambers of Commerce and Visitors Bureaus. The listings are provided alphabetically.

Additionally, a keyword search using a major search engine will lead you to Asian-American Chambers of Commerce around the United States as well as other ethnic Chambers in various parts of the country.

Once you have checked out the Chamber resources, you should consider contacts that share an alma mater with you. This common link can create a strong bond.

Sincerity is a prized trait when networking. The individual that you are communicating with needs to know that you sincerely want to hear his or her advice and that you appreciate the time that is being spent giving it.

College and High School Alumni

Many colleges offer both current students and alumni access to their career service centers and alumni contacts. You will probably need to speak directly with the staff of your college's center to find out how to get in touch with graduates. The easiest way to find a contact for your career center is to check out your school's website.

Also, check out the alumni association services of your school. Some schools offer alumni directories online as part of an alumni association membership.

JobWeb
http://www.jobweb.com/article.aspx?id=648
This section of JobWeb's site offers links to career centers around the United States and internationally.

For high school alumni, a quick call to a guidance counselor at the school may be of help. The counselors are often aware of websites, clubs, or networks that graduates may have established. Another option is to use a web service that specializes in helping alumni contact one another.

Two examples of these sites are

Classmates.com
http://www.classmates.com

Reunion.com
http://www.reunion.com

These sites contain information on millions of high school alumni. Classmates.com even offers college, work, and military contact services. Be aware that the initial sign-up is free, but communicating with fellow alumni may cost you. Please exercise caution with these sites and read all the fine print.

Military Contacts
Military Brats Registry
http://www.military-brats.com/
This website is the place to connect with others who grew up in military families. In addition to an online search feature, the site provides detailed information on finding both military and other persons who you are seeking. You can even go shopping for some

> You should approach your networking contacts seeking information and further contacts. It is not wise to start an initial conversation with the first words out of your mouth being "What jobs do you have for me?".

military brat merchandise or listen to podcasts from others who grew up military.

Business Alumni Associations

Do not overlook the possibility that a former employer (generally the larger employers) may have spawned an alumni association. Job-Hunt.org offers a listing of business and military alumni association links. You may also want to use a search engine to do a quick query for the company name and alumni to see what is available.

Job-Hunt.org

http://www.job-hunt.org/employer_alumni_networking.shtml

Some examples of associations that are listed on this section of the Job-Hunt.org site are Arthur Anderson Alumni, Army Career and Alumni Program, HP Alumni Association, Marine Corps League, Proctor and Gamble Alumni, Walgreens Alumni Association, and Women Marines Association.

Hewlett-Packard's Alumni

http://www.hpalumni.org/

Hewlett-Packard's Alumni Site is a good example of what these former employer networks can offer.

Professional Associations for Your Field of Interest

Associations exist for almost any profession that you can name. Participation in these associations can provide opportunities to learn more about your profession, network with potential employers, and have access to specialized job banks. Listed next is a print publication and some websites that can help you track down associations related to your field or fields of interest.

Print Resource
Swartout, Kristy. *Encyclopedia of Associations: National Organizations of the U.S.* 44th ed. Vol. 1. Farmington Hills, MI: Thomson Gale.

This publication is the big daddy of association listings with more than 135,000 nonprofit membership organizations noted. Check with your local library to see if they have this resource available as a multi-volume set of books or on CD. Keep your eyes peeled at your library for the *Encyclopedia of Associations: Regional, State, and Local Organizations* set as well.

American Society of Association Executives Website
http://www.asaecenter.org/
For locating relevant trade associations, check out this site's searchable database called Gateway to Associations. This resource is found under the "People and Groups" drop down menu, under the "Directories" section. You can filter your search by geographic location and keyword.

Internet Public Library
http://www.ipl.org/div/aon/
This site is designed as a public library by and for Internet users. The "Associations on the Net" section lists associations by major

career categories. You can scroll down until you find the associations that best meet your needs.

Weddles Association List
http://www.weddles.com/associations/index.cfm
This section of the Weddle's site lists several thousand associations worldwide by their occupational/industry focus.

Yahoo! Directory
http://dir.yahoo.com/Business_and_Economy/Organizations/
Under the "Business and Economy>Organizations" section of this major search engine, you will find more than 11,000 organizations including professional and trade associations that are listed by sub-category.

Speaking of associations, some examples of the range of trade and professional associations operating in the business world today include

American Advertising Federation
http://www.aaf.org/

American Bankers Association
http://www.aba.com/

American Chemical Society
http://www.acs.org/

American Hotel & Lodging Association
http://www.ahla.com/

American Insurance Association
http://www.aiadc.org/AIAdotNet/

American Management Association
http://www.amanet.org/index.htm

American Society of Interior Designers
http://www.asid.org/

American Trucking Associations
http://www.truckline.com/

Association of Fundraising Professionals
http://www.afpnet.org/

Direct Marketing Association
http://www.the-dma.org/

eMarketing Association
http://www.emarketingassociation.com/

Household Goods Forwarders Association of America
http://www.hhgfaa.org/

International Association of Administrative Professionals
http://www.iaap-hq.org/

Meeting Professionals International
http://www.mpiweb.org/

National Association for the Self-Employed
http://www.nase.org/

National Association of Home Builders
http://www.nahb.com/

National Association of Professional Pet Sitters
http://www.petsitters.org/

National Association of Realtors
http://www.realtor.com/

National Association of Women Business Owners
http://www.nawbo.org/

National Athletic Trainers' Association
http://www.nata.org/

National Black MBA Association
http://www.nbmbaa.org/

National Mail Order Association
http://www.nmoa.org/

National Pest Management Association
http://www.pestworld.org/

National Retail Federation
http://www.nrf.com/

National Small Business Association
http://www.nsba.biz/

National Society of Hispanic MBAs
http://www.nshmba.org/

Public Relations Society of America
http://www.prsa.org/

Society for Human Resource Management
http://www.shrm.org/

Steel Erectors Association of America
http://www.seaa.net/

The Association of Support Professionals
http://www.asponline.com/

United States Ombudsman Association
http://www.usombudsman.org/

United States Parachute Association
http://www.uspa.org/

United States Telecom Association
http://www.usta.org/

United States Tour Operators Association
http://www.ustoa.com/

Better Business Bureau Chapters

The Better Business Bureau through its chapters can provide a great source for networking contacts.

BBB

http://www.bbb.org/

The national Better Business Bureau and its chapters across the United States offer information on business members and their track records, as well as, serve as watchdogs for the consumer regarding Internet, work-at-home offers, etc. . . The national homepage offers links to local/regional bureaus homepages where you can find detailed information about a number of businesses.

Online Networking Organizations and Clubs

When networking, you may want to explore online networking organizations and clubs. This category of sites on the Internet is rapidly exploding. These websites offer opportunities to network with people around the world via an initial Internet contact. They may be helpful in garnering you contacts, but also can be a major time eater. Allocate yourself only a small, fixed amount of time here. Some sample sites include

Business Network International

http://www.bni.com/

BNI offers users the opportunity to meet other businesspersons and to develop a system of business referrals and contacts. From the organization's international website, you can search for your closest local chapter and sign up for a free networking-related e-newsletter.

Ecademy
http://www.ecademy.com/
This social networking site focuses on business people and now has over 100,000 members worldwide. The website is geared towards connecting people in order to enhance business activities.

Friendster
http://www.friendster.com/
Friendster boasts over 40 million members. You must register to use this site's services.

MySpace
http://www.myspace.com/
This social networking site is growing in popularity with people of all ages. Use a keyword search to locate others with similar occupational interests.

Orkut
http://www.orkut.com
Orkut is a social network site offered by Google.

Other well-trafficked social networking sites include FaceBook, MSN Groups, and Yahoo! Groups. More and more business networking opportunities seem to be developing on these sites all the time.

If you develop your own page on a social networking site, *be sure that the content is appropriate for a potential employer to see.* Many individuals doing the hiring now do a search on the web to see what they can find out about the job candidates. A picture of you face down in a bush after a hard night of partying may not impress your potential boss.

Community Clubs, Business Groups, and Volunteer Organizations

More great sources of networking contacts as well as opportunities for long-term community involvement may be found by checking out a variety of community organizations.

Business and Professional Women (BPW)/USA
http://www.bpwusa.org
Headquarters: 1900 M Street, NW, Suite 310, Washington, D.C. 20036
BPW focuses on providing career advancement support, personal and professional connections, as well as, work strategies for women. BPW is also active in Washington D.C. keeping working women's issues in the forefront. Plus, the website offers a local organization directory and an online job board created with women and veterans in mind. You can set up a job agent to e-mail you jobs that meet your criteria.

Civitan International
http://www.civitaninternational.com
Headquarters: P.O. Box 130744, Birmingham, Alabama 35213-0744

Civitan International is committed to improving the lives of children and adults with developmental disabilities. The organization supports vocational programs, camps, and research into Alzheimer's, Autism, and Cerebral Palsy through its International Research Center. Local clubs are involved in a range of service projects. This website offers a club directory.

General Federation of Women's Clubs (GFWC)
http://www.gfwc.org
Headquarters: 1734 N Street, NW, Washington, D.C. 20036-2990
The GFWC is a large women's service organization with a membership that supports the arts, natural resource preservation, education, civic involvement, and much more. Local clubs put their service efforts towards issues that affect their communities and nations. The website offers a clubs' links section.

Kiwanis International
http://www.kiwanis.org
Headquarters: 3636 Woodview Trace, Indianapolis, IN, 46268-3196
This global organization's motto is "Serving the Children of the World". Local clubs focus on service in support of children and young adults and other community projects. Internationally, the club has been instrumental in the march towards the eradication of Iodine Deficiency Disorders. Also, this website offers a local club directory.

Lions Clubs International

http://www.lionsclubs.org

Headquarters: 300 W. 22nd Street, Oak Brook, IL 60523-8842

This global organization with the mission "We Serve", takes on issues such as blindness, drug abuse prevention, and diabetes awareness. You may be familiar with the organization through its collection and recycling of eyeglasses for distribution in developing countries. At this website, you will also find a club directory.

Pilot International

http://www.pilotinternational.org

Headquarters: P.O. Box 4844, Macon, GA 31208

This volunteer service organization's activities focus on making a positive difference in the areas of brain-related disorders, such as Alzheimer's disease, chemical dependency, traumatic brain injuries, developmental, emotional, and mental disabilities. Check out the website's club directory.

Rotary International

http://www.rotary.org

Headquarters: One Rotary Center, 1560 Sherman Avenue, Evanston, IL 60201

Rotary is a worldwide organization of business and professional leaders that provides humanitarian service, encourages high ethical standards in all vocations, and helps build goodwill and peace in the world. Polio eradication, youth exchange, and fostering inter-national understanding are among the activities for which the orga-nization is known. Find a Rotary club near you through the online club directory. In many towns, Rotary clubs have large membership that meet frequently. These clubs tend to have members from a diversity of professions.

Sertoma
http://www.sertoma.org
Headquarters: 1912 E. Meyer Blvd., Kansas City, MO 64132
The combination of the three words "Service to Mankind" forms the interesting name of this organization. The group's primary focus is assisting people with speech, hearing, and language disorders. Local clubs also focus on community service projects such as promoting democracy and assisting with youth needs. Find your local club through the national website.

The American Legion
http://www.legion.org
Headquarters: P.O. Box 1055, Indianapolis, IN, 46206
Chartered in 1919 by Congress, The American Legion is a community-service oriented veteran's organization. To join, individuals must have served at least one day of active military service during specifics periods of time coinciding with United States foreign military engagements. Check out the post directory online and the link to the American Legion Career Center located on Monster. com.

Caution: Service to your community is contagious.

Toastmasters International
http://www.toastmasters.org/
Headquarters: P.O. Box 9052, Mission Viejo, CA 92690
Toastmasters is focused on honing members' speaking skills and polishing up leadership skills. Find a Toastmasters Club near you through this website.

United States Junior Chamber (Jaycees)
http://www.usjaycees.org
Headquarters: P.O. Box 7, Tulsa, OK 74102-0007
This organization gives individuals aged 18 to 40 the opportunity to develop personal and leadership skills through service to others. Nationally, the organization has raised millions of dollars for the Muscular Dystrophy Association and the March of Dimes. Countless local service projects take place on an ongoing basis in communities throughout the nation. The website features a club directory.

Zonta International
http://www.zonta.org
Headquarters: 557 West Randolph Street, Chicago, IL 60661
Founded in 1919, Zonta International is a service organization for executives in business that works to advance the status of women worldwide. Members participate in service projects as well, and the organization offers scholarship opportunities for women. Be sure and check this website for a club directory.

Nonprofit Networking

For those of you who have an interest in nonprofit businesses, establishing a contact within your local United Way chapter can be very helpful. Personnel at the United Way offices are generally very familiar with a number of nonprofits in a given region, even if organizations are not United Way members. They are often aware of jobs that are available throughout the region.

United Way of America
http://national.unitedway.org/
Headquarters: 701 N. Fairfax Street, Alexandria, VA 22314
The United Way system includes approximately 1,350 community-based United Way organizations. Each organization is independent, separately incorporated, and governed by local volunteers. United Way works with businesses, community development corporations, financial institutions, government agencies, schools, and many more entities. United Way also provides a 2-1-1 System to match community members with the human services that they may need.

When networking, keep a detailed record of each contact so that you can go back and refer to the information provided by that person as often as needed. Also, always try to obtain two to three additional contact names from each person that you speak with in order to grow your network.

Generally, the quickest way to reach a networking contact is to phone him or her. A short note in the mail or e-mail letting the contact know who you are and why you will be calling is very helpful. Some contacts will respond rapidly to an e-mail.

Additionally, you may want to look into the following:

Independent Sector's Member List
http://www.independentsector.org/members/memberlist. asp?orderVar=company_sort
Independent Sector's member list offers web links to a number of nonprofits and foundations. Also, a "JobLink" section is available with openings posted for some Independent Sector member organizations.

Once you have put together your list of potential contacts using the suggested sources offered throughout this chapter, you are ready to begin contacting these individuals. One of the keys to a smooth job search is to stay organized. Keep a written record as mentioned above and leave yourself a box to check off when you send a thank you note to each contact.

You can immediately set yourself apart from the crowd through your follow up. So many people neglect this powerful opportunity to show appreciation. You will be remembered for your efforts.

On the next two pages, you will find examples of a networking contact sheet and of a networking e-mail/letter. These examples can be adapted to meet your individual needs.

Networking Contact Sheet

Name of Contact_____

Company or Other_____

Phone Number_____

E-mail Address_____

Mailing Address_____

_____

When Contacted_____

Information Received_____

_____

_____

Other Contacts Suggested
Name(s), Company and Way to Contact

_____

_____

_____

❑ Thank You Note Sent

Networking E-mail/Letter

Month Day, Year

Ms. Ann Jones
Best Product Ever Company
100 Smith Street
Anytown, State Zip Code

Dear Ms. Jones:

I am a marketing and communications professional
who has recently relocated to Anytown (who
has recently graduated from Great College). I would
greatly appreciate your advice about the marketing
and communications fields in this area. Also, I
would like to speak with you about any current
career opportunities that you are aware of in
Anytown and the surrounding region.

Thank you in advance for your time and
consideration. I look forward to speaking with you
and will give you call next Friday. If you would like
to reach me before that time, I can be contacted at
xxx-xxxx or via e-mail at GeorgeJay@ipa.com.

Sincerely,
George Jay

CHAPTER TWO

Ah! Smell the Ink!

You may wonder why I would put the print section before discussing online job boards and search tools. The simple truth is that for medium and small-sized cities and towns, the good old newspaper and other regional print publications are some of the most valuable sources of information. You can gather all sorts of good leads from daily and weekly papers, business, and social publications.

The Scoop on Newspapers and Classifieds in the Internet Age

The classifieds job ads are probably one of the most misunderstood and misused job tools in existence today. Some people make the mistake of relying on the classifieds too much, and some individuals do not make use of them as they should. A lot of misuse is due to people's perceptions of how well the classifieds work for others.

I think the crowd that rarely uses classifieds has heard the big city horror stories of thousands of people applying for the same advertised jobs. Their resumes get lost in the piles and piles of resumes sent in, and they never really know whether their resumes were even received. They are competing against so many people with similar skills sets that they feel they hardly stand a chance anyway.

In some big city settings, scenarios such as the above probably are not uncommon. The medium to small-sized markets are a different ballgame though. In these markets, fewer people see the classifieds and even fewer have the skill sets needed for jobs that require very specialized knowledge.

I know the classifieds are worth your time based upon my personal experience. I have scored several good mid-level professional jobs from these ads.

However, I do have some words of caution to the classifieds-are-the-only-thing-I-use crowd. Only small portions of available jobs are advertised in the classifieds. Many jobs are not ever publicly advertised and are instead filled through networking and referrals. Include classified ads in your job strategy, but be sure to use networking and the other job tools for a well-rounded search.

The Sports Page, Your Secret Weapon?

The classified section is not the only section worth checking out for your job search. Almost every section of the paper can offer you valuable information.

Front page and local section

Scan for information about new or expanding businesses, the names of business leaders and government officials, and any news in your interest area that might provide you with leads. For example, I noticed in our daily paper that a gentleman had won a national award for his growing medical supply business. I wrote a letter to him congratulating him on the award and asked him to keep me in mind should any openings arise at his company. Within two weeks he called me to schedule an interview for a marketing position that he had available.

Lifestyle/Society

Aside from being an entertaining section of the paper, you can use the articles here to learn about the movers and shakers in town. Take special note of names that you see mentioned frequently in the society section and the hobbies or causes supported by these power players.

Sports

You will want to study this section if you are looking for a sports-related job. Even if you are not, knowing what is going on in local sports can be a big plus. Sports are like the weather, they make for great small talk. Also, you may find out about local community teams who need help with skills you have– leading to more net-working opportunities as well.

Club/Activities Listings

Find out about organizations that you can become involved in and networking opportunities.

Special Sections or Inserts

These special additions to the paper can be gold mines of information. For example, the local daily where I live publishes each of two area Chamber of Commerce membership directories. These publications list company contact names and address information.

Although this may sound old-fashion, I recommend that you get your hands on the actual newspaper or its microfilm/microfiche version. Yes, I know, this means a trip to the local library or purchasing a subscription; but it is well worth it. Online versions of papers continue to improve, but they are still no substitute for the actual paper version. Ads or announcements not found online may provide you with great leads.

Finding Your News

The easiest way to find out what newspapers are in your region of interest is to use an online search engine. In addition, some Internet directories that you may want to check out to find newspapers of interest include

NewsLink

http://newslink.org/news.html

NewsLink includes thousands of links to newspapers, as well as, a break down by daily, weekly, business, and alternative. Also, links to radio and television by geographic area can be found here.

NewsVoyager

http://www.newspaperlinks.com/voyager.cfm

I like this site because it is easy to navigate and quickly takes you to the information that you desire.

Onlinenewspapers.com

http://www.onlinenewspapers.com/

This site offers links to newspapers from around the world, broken down by region.

Refdesk.com

http://www.refdesk.com/paper.html

Refdesk.com offers links to newspapers in the U.S. and around the world. Additionally, this site offers all sorts of links to reference materials including online dictionaries, business, and people searches.

SmallTownPapers

http://www.smalltownpapers.com

I like this site, not because of its volume of information, but because it contains entire newspapers scanned in for reading. Who knows, you may be moving to an area covered by one of the more than 250 small town newspapers scanned into this site.

Who Says That Business and Social Publications Don't Mix

While we are on the subject of print publications, I encourage you to check out any regional business or society publications that cover your job search area. These publications often offer information beyond what is found in the newspaper. Additionally, these publications offer special editions from time to time. Find out what is available by using the following resources:

AccessMyLibrary
http://www.accessmylibrary.com/topics/business
This section of this site run by Thomas Gale offers a lengthy list of business publications.

The Alliance of Area Business Publications
http://www.bizpubs.org
This website offers links to multiple publications that provide regional business news.

Bizjournals
http://www.bizjournals.com/
Bizjournals is the new media division of American City Business Journals, the nation's largest publisher of metropolitan business newspapers. It operates the websites for each of the company's print business journals.

The following is a brief list of some regional and statewide publications available in the United States.

Alabama Living
Alaska Journal of Commerce
Albuquerque The Magazine
Buffalo Spree Magazine
Cape Cod Life Magazine
Central Penn Business Journal
Colorado Homes and Lifestyles

Desert Living

Entertainment Fort Smith

Evansville Living

Florida Trend

Gulfscapes

Gulfshore Life

Hartford Business Journal

Hill Country Sun

Lehigh Valley Style

Mainebiz

Mississippi Business Journal

Mountain Echo

New Hampshire Business Review

North Valley Magazine

Northwest Arkansas Business Journal

Oklahoma Living Magazine

Savannah Magazine

Spokane Journal of Business

The Business Journal of the Greater Triad Area (Greensboro)

The Iowan

Today's Arizona Woman

Traverse

Utah Business

Western Carolina Business Journal

Wind River Country

Worcester Business Journal

CHAPTER THREE

All That's Fit to Publish on the Net

As of September 2007, according to Netcraft News, there were more than 135 million websites on the Internet.[1] Technorati, a company specializing in "World *Live Web*," indicated on its website in fall 2007, that it was tracking more than 105 million blogs.[2]

What do these numbers mean for you? A lot of useful information is out there on the Internet. However, there is also a lot of stuff that can take you off on a tangent, eat up your time, and keep you from getting where you need to be—which is why a carefully targeted online job search strategy is a necessity.

The Online Majors

Let's start with some of the "biggie" job search websites. One issue I see with these sites is that many job seekers spend hours of their search time here when these sites may not be specialized enough for the smaller city dweller. When it comes to the medium-sized cities and towns, some search sites do not cover these areas as much as the larger metropolitan areas. To save yourself time, *put the search agents to work for you.* Specify what types of positions that you are looking for and the sites will bring results directly to you.

Let's look at some examples of large online job sites:

Monster.com
http://www.monster.com
This site is a good place to start a search, but you will find that geographic areas outside the big cities are often grouped by region. For example, California-Central Coast, Georgia-Northeast, and West Virginia-Southern. You can narrow areas down by zip code, which helps; but sometimes a very specific search still brings up jobs outside your target area.

Yahoo! HotJobs
http://www.hotjobs.com
Use the keyword, industry, and city job search features that are available to narrow down your job hunt. You can get pretty specific geographically and sort by location as needed. As with other sites, job search agents are available.

America's Job Exchange
http://www.americasjobexchange.com/
AJE offers similar national labor exchange services to those that America's JobBank provided for a number of years. For example, the site allows you to find a CareerOne Stop center near you, as well as, maps of job-related resources in your area including community colleges. Also, you can hook into all the other resources under the CareerOneStop suite including America's CareerInfoNet and the Department of Defense Job Site.

CareerBuilder.com

http://www.careerbuilder.com

This site offers an easy to use and geographic specific search feature. Results tend to show a lot of national listings, so be sure to sort results by location; and then drill down your search as needed. You may also search by company, industry, or by a specific job category.

Be sure to be very specific when setting up your job alert agent. You can check a box to indicate that you would like no national or regional listings posted in your results.

Indeed

http://www.indeed.com

This job search engine compiles results from many different sites and brings them together in one list. You can drill down pretty specifically geographically. This site can be a good time saver.

In addition to the job search features, you can find links to information regarding specific trainings and certifications. Additionally, details about occupational licensing requirements for each state are available. You may also want to check out the hotlink to the military transition portal or the resume tutorial.

With hundreds, if not thousands, of job search sites out there, narrowing down your focus is essential. The more specific that you can be about what you are looking for, the quicker you are likely to find the results you need.

Another site of interest is JobCentral.com.

http://www.jobcentral.com

This site is a product of the DirectEmployers Association, a non-profit group of U.S. companies. This site is easy to use and you can narrow down your search geographically. I saw some listings here that I had not seen elsewhere. Maybe, it is because of the good results layout.

Regional Job Sites

These sites specialize in the job market in specific geographic areas. They concentrate on cultivating relationships with employers in those particular areas and therefore may be first to post particular job listings in your area. Some sites to check out include

RegionalHelpWanted.com

http://regionalhelpwanted.com/info/sitelist_domains.cfm?SN=1

More than 320 RegionalHelpWanted sites are now available for areas in the U.S. and Canada. The link above will lead you to the list of sites available. Be aware that when sorting through results on particular sites you may have to pass over some national ads.

Jobing.com

http://www.jobing.com

This site covers a relatively small number of medium-sized to larger areas. Job listings are for selected locations in Alabama, Arizona, Southern California, Colorado, Florida, Nevada, New Mexico, Southern New England, and Texas.

JobCircle.com

http://www.jobcircle.com

This well-organized regional site offers listing for jobs in Southeastern Pennsylvania and nearby areas in Connecticut, the District of Columbia, Delaware, Ohio, Maryland, New York, New Jersey, Pennsylvania, and Virginia. You can narrow your search down to within ten miles of your zip code in these areas. The website also offers a regional events calendar that can be brought up by zip code and an interesting employer profile section.

LocalCareers.com

http://www.localcareers.com

The website offers searches for states across the U.S., but cannot drill down to local cities easily. The e-mail search agent that the site offers is a good option. Also, you may want to look at the listing of career fairs.

State Employment Offices, Dept. of Labor, Commissions, and More

Each state has its own site or sites to assist with job searching. On these sites, you will find job banks with private and public sector openings and information about job search assistance in your area.

Many states have job search and employment centers located in a number of communities. These local centers' personnel can provide you with lots of valuable information and assistance if you will let them know what you need help with and stay in touch with them frequently.

Job Search by State

Alabama
Alabama JobLink
http://joblink.alabama.gov/

Alaska
Alaska Job Center Network
http://www.jobs.state.ak.us/

Arizona
Arizona Workforce Informer and Career Center
http://www.workforce.az.gov/

Arkansas
Arkansas Job Link
http://www.arjoblink.arkansas.gov/

California
CalJobs
http://www.caljobs.ca.gov/

Colorado
Colorado Workforce Center
http://www.connectingcolorado.com

Connecticut
CT JobCentral
http://www.jobcentral.org/ct/

Delaware
Delaware Joblink
https://joblink.delaware.gov/ada/default.cfm

District of Columbia
Department of Employment Services DC Networks
http://www.dcnetworks.org/

Florida
Employ Florida
http://www.employflorida.com/

Georgia
Georgia Dept. of Labor's Job Information System
http://www.dol.state.ga.us/js/

Hawaii
HireNet Hawaii
https://www.hirenethawaii.com/default.asp

Idaho
IdahoWorks
http://www.idahoworks.org/

Illinois
Illinois Skills Match
http://www.illinoisskillsmatch.com/

Indiana
Indiana's Workforce Development
http://www.in.gov/dwd/

Iowa
IowaJobs
http://www.iowajobs.org/

Kansas
Kansas JobLink
http://www.kansasjoblink.com

Kentucky
Office of Employment and Training
http://www.desky.org/

Louisiana
Louisiana Works
http://www.ldol.state.la.us/

Maine
CareerCenter
http://www.mainecareercenter.com/

Maryland
Maryland Workforce Exchange
http://www.mwejobs.com/

Massachusetts
Massachusetts Dept. of Workforce Development JobQuest
http://web.detma.org/JobSeeker/CM1.asp

Michigan
Michigan Talent Bank
http://www.michworks.org/

Minnesota
Minnesota's Job Bank
http://www.mnworks.org/

Mississippi
Mississippi Dept. of Employment Security
http://www.mdes.ms.gov/

Missouri
GreatHires.org
http://www.greathires.org/

Montana
Jobs.mt.gov
http://jobs.mt.gov/

Nebraska
Nebraska JobLink
http://nejoblink.dol.state.ne.us/

Nevada
Nevada JobConnect
http://www.nevadajobconnect.com/

New Hampshire
NH Works
http://www.nhworks.org/

New Hampshire Employment Security Job Match System
http://www.nhes.state.nh.us/itsweb/

New Jersey
Workforce New Jersey
http://lwd.dol.state.nj.us/labor/wnjpin/wnjpin_index.html

New Mexico
New Mexico Workforce Connection
http://www.jobs.state.nm.us/

New York
Workforce NY
http://www.labor.state.ny.us/

North Carolina
Employment Security Commission's North Carolina's Job
Bank
http://www.ncesc.com/individual/jis/jisMain.asp

North Dakota
Job Service North Dakota
http://www.jobsnd.com/

Ohio
Ohio Workforce 411
http://www.ohioworkforce411.gov/jobseekers/

Oklahoma
Oklahoma Job Link
https://servicelink.oesc.state.ok.us/ada/default.cfm

Oregon
WorkSource Oregon
http://www.employment.oregon.gov/

Pennsylvania
Pennsylvania CareerLink
http://www.pacareerlink.state.pa.us

Job Resources by State Continued. . .

Rhode Island
NetWorkri
http://www.networkri.org/

South Carolina
South Carolina's Job Bank
http://www.sces.org/Jobs/

South Dakota
South Dakota Department of Labor
http://www.state.sd.us/applications/LD01DOL/

Tennessee
Department of Labor & Workforce Development
http://www.state.tn.us/labor-wfd/mainfindajob.html

Texas
WorkInTexas.com
http://www.workintexas.com

Utah
Utah's Job Connection
http://jobs.utah.gov/jobseeker/

Vermont
Vermont JobLink
http://www.vermontjoblink.com/

Virginia
VaWorkConnect.com
https://www.vawc.virginia.gov/

Washington
Access Washington
http://access.wa.gov/employment/getajob.aspx

West Virginia
WV Gov
http://www.wv.gov/sec.aspx?pgID=22

Wisconsin
Wisconsin JobNet Job Search
http://jobnet.wisconsin.gov/JobNet/

Wyoming
Wyomingatwork.com
http://www.wyomingatwork.com/

Other

Guam

Department of Labor Job Bank

http://www.guamdol.net/component/option,com_jobline/

Itemid,213/

The IRS is Looking Pretty Good . . . Explore Opportunities in Government

From big cities to small towns, government is a part of life. Getting drivers' licenses, obtaining voter registration cards, paying taxes, and many more activities bring you in contact with government. Take advantage of this fact by exploring job openings in local, state, and federal government. Government positions may not always offer the top pay, but the benefits (at least for now) are pretty darn good.

Jobs at the local level

To find out about city government positions, contact the human resources director or check out the city's website. In really small places, the mayor or town administrator may also be the HR person. Some departments that may fall under city government include animal control, the fire department, police department, planning office, parks and recreation, public works, and transportation.

County or parish government

Depending on where you live, you may find a host of different jobs related to the county or parish level of government. The accounting office, health department, highway maintenance, information technology, and the sheriff's office are just some of the entities you will find at this level. As with city government, contact the county's human resources office. You may also want to check out

FirstGov.gov
http://www.firstgov.gov/
By searching through the US Government's Official Web Portal, you will find links to local governments, the National Association of Counties, and the National League of Cities.

State and Local Government on the Net
http://www.statelocalgov.net
This site offers links to many state, county, and local government websites.

Jobs at the State Level

Speaking of states, a number of different types of jobs exist at this level of government. Contrary to popular belief, not all state jobs are located in the capitol city. You just have to do a little research to see what is available near you.

A great place to start is with each state's human resources or state employment office. To make things easy for you, I have listed a web link and phone number for each office. Note on phone numbers that the main office may direct you to a job center near you.

State Employment Sites

Alabama
State Personnel Department
http://www.personnel.state.al.us/
P: 334-242-3389

Alaska
Workplace Alaska
http://notes4.state.ak.us/
P: 800-587-0430 (Statewide toll-free number)
P: 907-465-4095 (Juneau and out-of-state calls)

Arizona
Arizona State Jobs
http://www.azstatejobs.gov/
P: 602-542-5482

Arkansas
Arkansas Government Jobs
http://www.ark.org/arstatejobs/
P: 501-682-2121

California
State Personnel Board
http://www.spb.ca.gov/employment/
P: 916 653-1705

Colorado

Dept. of Personnel & Administration

http://www.gssa.state.co.us/announce/

Job+Announcements.nsf/$about?OpenAbout

P: 303-866-3000

Connecticut

Department of Administrative Services

http://www.das.state.ct.us/exam/

P: 860-713-5205

Delaware

Employment Link

http://www.delawarestatejobs.com/

P: 302-739-5458

Florida

People First!

https://peoplefirst.myflorida.com/logon.htm

P: 877-562-7287

Georgia

The Job Site

http://thejobsite.org/

P: 404-232-3515

Hawaii
Department of Human Resources Development
http://www.hawaii.gov/hrd/main/esd/
P: 808-587-1111

Idaho
Division of Human Resources
http://www.dhr.idaho.gov/
P: 208-334-2263

Illinois
Central Management Services
http://www.illinois.gov/jobs/
P: 217-782-7100

Indiana
State Personnel Department
http://www.in.gov/jobs/
P: 317-232-0200

Iowa
Department of Administrative Services
http://das.hre.iowa.gov/state_jobs.html
P: 515-281-3087

Kansas
Division of Personnel Services
http://www.jobs.ks.gov
P: 785-296-4278

Kentucky
Personnel Cabinet
http://personnel.ky.gov/
P: 502-564-8030

Louisiana
Department of State Civil Service
http://www.dscs.state.la.us/
P: 866-783-5462

Maine
Bureau of Human Resources
http://www.maine.gov/statejobs/
P: 207-624-7800

Maryland
Department of Budget and Management
http://www.dbm.maryland.gov/ (Look for "Job Seekers"
section on this home page)
P: 800-705-3493

Massachusetts
Human Resources Division
http://ceo.hrd.state.ma.us/
P: 617-727-3555

Michigan
Department of Civil Service
http://www.michigan.gov/mdcs/
P: 517-373-3030

Minnesota
Department of Employee Relations
http://www.doer.state.mn.us/employment.htm
P: 800-657-3974

Mississippi
Department of Employment Security
http://www.mississippi.gov/index.jsp (And click on the
"Working in Mississippi" button on the sidebar)
P: 601-321-6000

Missouri
Office of Administration
http://www.mo.gov/mo/stjobs.htm
P: 573-751-4162

Montana
Mt.gov-State Personnel Division
http://mt.gov/statejobs/statejobs.asp
P: 406-444-3871

Nebraska
DAS State Personnel
http://www.das.state.ne.us/personnel/nejobs/per.htm
P: 402-471-2075

Nevada
Department of Personnel
http://dop.nv.gov/fshome.html
P: 775-684-0150 (Northern Nevada)
P: 702-486-2900 (Southern Nevada)

New Hampshire
Department of Administrative Services
http://www.nh.gov/hr/employmentlisting.html
P: 603-271-3262

New Jersey
New Jersey Department of Personnel
http://www.state.nj.us/personnel/jobs/
P: 609-292-4144

New Mexico
State Personnel Office
http://www.spo.state.nm.us/
P: 505-476-7759

New York
New York State Department of Labor
http://www.labor.state.ny.us/
P: 518-457-9000

North Carolina
Office of State Personnel
http://www.osp.state.nc.us/jobs/
P: 919-807-4800

North Dakota
Job Service North Dakota
http://www.jobsnd.com/seekers/
P: 701-328-2825

Ohio
Ohio.Gov
http://statejobs.ohio.gov/
P: 614-466-6947

State employment is often stable employment with good benefits.

Oklahoma
Oklahoma Employment Security Commission
http://www.oesc.state.ok.us/
P: 405-557-7100

Oregon
Employment Department
http://www.employment.oregon.gov/
P: 800-237-3710

Pennsylvania
Pennsylvania State Civil Service Commission
http://www.scsc.state.pa.us/
P: 717-783-3058

Rhode Island
Human Resources Outreach & Diversity Office
http://www.dlt.ri.gov/JobsRI/
P: 401-222-6397

South Carolina
Office of Human Resources
http://ohrweb.ohr.state.sc.us/OHR/OHR-applicant.phtm
P: 803-734-9080

South Dakota
The Bop Web

South Dakota Continued. . .
http://www.state.sd.us/jobs/
P: 605-773-3148

Tennessee
Tennessee.Gov
http://www.tennesseeanytime.org/government/
employment.html
P: 615-741-4841

Texas
WorkInTexas.com
http://www.twc.state.tx.us/jobs/job.html
P: 800-832-2829

Utah
Department of Human Resources Management
https://statejobs.utah.gov/
P: 801-538-3025

Vermont
Vermont Department of Human Resources
http://www.vermontpersonnel.org/
P: 800-640-1657

State employees range from accountants to zoologists.
If you can dream it, there very may be a state position
that exists for that very profession.

Virginia
Virginia Jobs
http://jobs.state.va.us/
P: 804-225-2131

Washington
Employment Security Department
http://careers.wa.gov/
P: 360-664-1960

West Virginia
WV Division of Personnel
http://www.state.wv.us/admin/personnel/jobs/
P: 304-558-3950

Wisconsin
WiscJobs
http://wiscjobs.state.wi.us/public/
P: 608-266-1731

Wyoming
A & I Human Resources Division
http://personnel.state.wy.us/stjobs/
P: 307-777-7188

Or check State Employment Offices Section of Job-Hunt.org
http://www.job-hunt.org/

Federal Government Jobs

Do not overlook federal government positions as a possibility. Okay, I hear you saying, "In my small town there is no way." You never know, therefore, I am listing below a few official sites that I would recommend that you check out to find out about federal openings. Also, you may want to conduct a search for the web page of individual agencies if you have some in mind.

Beware of imposter websites that are trying to sell you "How to Get a Government Job" kits. I notice that these sites are a dime a dozen in cyberspace. Check with the Better Business Bureau to find out more information about a company's credibility. Try out the following legitimate sites:

USAJOBS

http://www.usajobs.opm.gov/

USAJOBS is the official job site of the United States Federal Government. You can search for jobs throughout the country and post your resume for federal job opportunities. A section of the site also offers leads to state and local government positions.

FedWorld.gov

http://www.fedworld.gov/

You may also want to check out FedWorld.gov. This website is run by the United States Department of Commerce. If you need to speak to someone in the division behind this site, call 703-605-6000.

Freelance and Speciality Career Sites

Some websites focus specifically on freelance and contract work. This work can offer flexibility in hours and conditions, but may require some trade-offs related to benefits such as healthcare and vacation pay. You may also have to do projects for multiple companies in order to make a living wage.

Do not fall for work at home advertisements that sound to good to be true, such as folding letters to earn a $1000 a week. Check with your local Better Business Bureau about any questionable work advertisements that you find. Work is work. If it sounds too easy, it is.

The following is a good site to check out:

Sologig.com
http://www.sologig.com
This website lists thousands of jobs available on a freelance and contract basis. You must register with the site to see listings. There is no cost for registration. To get preferential placement of your profile when employers search for talent and to see listings before non-paying members, you must pay a fairly hefty monthly fee. Start with the free service and see how that works for you.

The technology and health care sectors offer some of the strongest specialty job sites focused on specific career areas. Sites are available, though, for a variety of fields. Some helpful websites include

Broadcasting

National Alliance of State Broadcasters

http://www.careerpage.org/

At this site, you will find a job bank that you can sort geographically for broadcasting careers. Additionally, this website offers a section describing career positions in the industry.

TVJobs.com

http://www.tvjobs.com

On the homepage, you will find broadcast-related job openings and resource materials such as a salary database and a station index.

Chemistry

ACS Careers

http://chemistryjobs.acs.org/careerdev/

This resource is focused on chemistry, pharmaceutical, and biotech jobs. The American Chemical Society provides this site.

Engineering

Dice Engineering

http://www.dice.com/engineering/

You will find this division of Dice's site similar to the technology section. Listings are available in the categories of civil engineering, general engineering, industrial engineering, mechanical engineering, software engineering, and telecom engineering.

Healthcare

HealtheCareers

http://www.healthecareers.com

This job site is provided by a partnership of a variety of healthcare associations. Do not expect an overload of job search results, but you may luck out and find a job listing near you. Registration will be required to utilize the full resources of the site.

HealthcareSource.com

http://www.healthcaresource.com/

Search by state and selected job descriptions in healthcare fields. Additionally, you may search by facility if it is listed with this site.

HospitalWeb

http://neuro-www.mgh.harvard.edu/hospitalweb.shtml

HospitalWeb offers a pretty extensive listing of hospitals around the U.S. and globally. Many of the hospitals noted list their current job openings on their websites.

MedHunters.com

http://www.medhunters.com

You can search for allied health, nursing, physician, and other healthcare related positions here. Additionally, you can find a variety of relevant career articles at this site.

Interior Design

American Society of Interior Designers Job Bank

http://www.asid.org/Job+Bank.htm

Along with job listings, you can find information about continuing education opportunities, available awards and recognitions, and local chapters of this national association. Also, while here, pick up some tips on sustainable design.

Law Enforcement, Fire Fighting and Other Public Safety Jobs
FireRecruit.com
http://www.firerecruit.com/
For a monthly subscription fee, you can access listings for fire fighting and other fire career positions in 50 states. You will also find a testing tips section.

LawEnforcementJobs.com
http://lawenforcementjobs.com/
Through this site, you can access listings of law enforcement vacancies. Additionally, you can take advantage of interviewing advice and a salary database.

Officer.com
http://www.officer.com
Along with law enforcement news and numerous other useful features, this site offers a job openings section. Additionally, you can sign up for e-mail alerts when new job positions are posted.

911hotjobs.com
http://www.911hotjobs.com
At this location, you will find listings for jobs in law enforcement, fire, and EMS. Also, offered here are links to industry-related resources. A paid membership is required to view additional job postings above those easily accessed through the site. Approach a

paid membership with caution and be sure that you understand the fees and length of contract before enrolling.

Nonprofit
VolunteerMatch
http://www.volunteermatch.org/directory/
VolunteerMatch offers a directory of volunteer opportunities by zip code. You may find contacts that lead you to employment. This site is well organized and easy to use.

The NonProfit Times
http://www.nptjobs.com/search/
Look at the job section of the website for possible job opportunities in your state or neighboring states. Do not spend too much time here, but you never know when an opportunity might be available in your region.

Technology
Dice
http://www.dice.com
With this site, you can search in very specific geographic areas, as well as, expand out by state or area code. You can specify employment type, such as contract only. Additionally, you can click a box that will let you look at telecommuting jobs only or specify amount of travel time. Start broad and narrow in if possible. Set up a job alert e-mail to be sent to you to stay on top of the latest listings.

For more links to specific career job sites check out:

QuintCareers.com
http://www.quintcareers.com/indres.html
In the "Career and Job Resources-- by Industry" section, you will find numerous links to career specific job sites. Main categories range from Jobs in Academia, Teaching and Education to Jobs in Writing, Journalism, and Publishing.

Recruiters Network
http://www.recruitersnetwork.com
This site is a product of the Association of Internet Recruiting. The "Career Sites" directory under the Resource Center allows you to search by industry and location for job sites.

Jobs Sites That Focus on Where You Are in Life

Whole categories of job websites exist that focus on your stage of life. Whether you are still in college or have just graduated, an active or former member of the military, facing a disability or looking for a job later in life, you will find websites that address your situation.

College
AfterCollege
http://www.aftercollege.com/
This site offers listings of job opportunities for the new college

graduate. Sections of the site require a password and username available from the career centers of specific colleges and universities.

CampusCareerCenter.com
http://www.campuscareercenter.com/
CCC boasts a network consisting of about 2,200 career centers and a student representative program. CCC specializes in helping Fortune 500 companies recruit nationwide.

Career Opportunities for Students with Disabilities (COSD)
http://www.cosdonline.org/
COSD is a consortium of universities, U.S. Government agencies, and employers. The organization is focused on employment of college graduates with disabilities.

CollegeRecruiter.com
http://www.collegerecruiter.com/
This website focuses on job and internship searches, as well as, offers research tools for college students and recent grads.

JobWeb
http://www.jobweb.com/
JobWeb provides a website focused on career development and job search information for college students and new college graduates. The site is owned and sponsored by the National Association of Colleges and Employers (NACE). In addition to the job search tools found on the site, a career library is offered.

MonsterTrak

http://www.monstertrak.monster.com/

The focus of MonsterTrak, part of Monster.com, is helping college students and recent grads find jobs. Also, available through the site is a salary center and career guide.

Vault

http://www.vault.com

Many college career centers offer access to Vault, and its suite of resources. Vault features job search, as well as, tools for researching companies and salaries.

Military Transition

HireVetsFirst

http://www.hirevetsfirst.gov

This website offers lots of career resource materials specifically tailored to veterans.

Military Connection

http://www.militaryconnection.com/

Military Connection focuses on job opportunities for military

QuintCareers.com offers a section with links to a number of sites that focus on job transitioning for individuals moving from the military to a civilian workplace. In addition, this site offers a click through to a listing of books that focus on the move to civilian life.

personnel, listings of employers, information resources for all branches of service, and special military spouse materials.

VetJobs

http://www.vetjobs.com/

VetJobs offers assistance with job leads for those veterans already in the workforce, as well as, those individuals transitioning from active duty to civilian life.

50 Plus

Retired Brains

http://www.retiredbrains.com/

Through this website, you can find part-time, full-time, and temporary jobs for those who want to work after retirement.

RetirementJobs.com

http://www.retirementjobs.com/

This site specializes in job searches for individuals who are 50 or older. Along with the search feature, you will find a resource center.

Specialty Skills

Bilingual-Jobs.com

http://www.bilingual-jobs.com/

If you speak multiple languages, you may find job postings here.

ClearanceJobs.com

http://www.clearancejobs.com/

ClearanceJobs.com matches individuals that possess active Department of Defense, Department of State, and Department of Energy security clearances to employers.

ClearedConnections.com

http://www.clearedconnections.com/

Similar to the website above, ClearedConnections.com links job seekers with security clearance to employers who need them.

Diversity

Jobs4Diversity.com

http://www.jobs4diversity.com

This site is part of the LocalCareers.com Network. Job results may vary greatly depending on job title and geographic region searched.

LatPro.com

http://www.latpro.com

The website features jobs for Hispanic and bilingual job seekers. With registration, you can receive job alerts via e-mail.

Mailing Lists, Newsgroups, and the Latest Technology

Mailing lists on the Internet abound. By conducting a quick search, you may find some mailing lists with relevant job openings or job topics listed. Do not spend too much of your time here.

Sign up to receive the e-mail list postings that are appropriate and move on.

Catalist
http://www.lsoft.com/lists/listref.html
Browse any of the thousands of public LISTSERV lists on the Internet. You can search by interest area to help narrow down your search.

Tile.net
http://tile.net/lists/
Search for mailing lists and e-mail newsletters by keyword to help zoom in on information that may be relevant to you.

Craigslist
http://www.craigslist.org/about/cities.html
These local community forums generally have job sections where you may find some classified ads and potential networking contacts. (Note that these lists have been formed for mainly medium-sized cities and above.) Type the term Craigslist into your search engine along with your town name to see if there is a site that will work for you. Sites are available for cities such as: Albany, NY; Allentown, PA; Bakersfield, CA; El Paso, TX; Eugene, OR; Fort Myers, FL; Jackson, MS; Madison, WI; New Haven, CT; Richmond, VA; and Shreveport, LA.

A variety of websites are available to search for newsgroups that may offer information relevant to your job search. Newsgroups are essentially the holding areas for postings from a variety of different users on particular topics. Check out the following to search for newsgroups:

Google Groups
http://www.groups.google.com
At this site, you can search for newsgroups based upon keywords. Additionally, you can create your own group if you desire.

Speaking of groups, as I mentioned in an earlier chapter, social networking sites continue to grow at an amazing rate. These sites, such as Bebo, FaceBook, Friendster, LinkedIn, and MySpace are growing in popularity as ways for job seekers and employers to network and exchange information. Look for this trend to continue.

Some quick searches on MySpace show that companies such as Apple, Accenture, Gap, Microsoft, and Wendy's have spaces where the public can interact with employees. Also, MySpace and other social networking sites offer regional groups where you may find contacts that can help you. Do some quick searches, find resources that will be useful, and then move on.

Another emerging development is texting to find job openings. Some companies are now enabling job seekers to send text messages with specific information to receive job opening descriptions on their texting devices. This technology is rapidly developing; so keep your eye on it, but do not spend any significant amount of time on this method at this time.

Short Term Options to Consider

Often, you can find good short-term work and enhance your skills while looking for something more permanent. Below are some options to consider.

Apprenticeship

U.S. Department of Labor

http://bat.doleta.gov/bat.cfm

Opportunities are available to learn through both books and on the job training while generally earning a wage. Check out the U.S. Department of Labor's Bureau of Apprenticeship and Training Program Sponsor Database. You can search by state and by county.

Hourly

Snagajob.com

http://www.snagajob.com/

This site bills itself as the top choice for finding hourly employment. You can sign up to receive job postings by e-mail or create a profile for potential employers to review.

Seasonal

CoolWorks.com

http://www.coolworks.com

Find seasonal work ranging from a camp counselor to serving as a tour guide for a tour company. You can search for a variety of jobs by state or by type of position.

National Park Service

http://www.sep.nps.gov/

This site is focused on temporary positions and offers an online application. The website's listings may be good options if you live near a national park.

Service

AmeriCorps

http://www.americorps.org/

AmeriCorps is a network of local, state, and national service organizations that offer Americans opportunities for intensive service in the areas of health, education, environment, and public safety. Workers earn stipends and funding for continued education.

Substitute Teaching

Your Local School System(s)

Local websites or human resources offices

I have worked as a substitute teacher in several cities over the years while looking for a position in my field. I found subbing to be a great way to get out of the house for a while, but still have time in the afternoon to make calls and network. Also, with substitute teaching, I had the option of not working on the days that I had interviews or something else going on.

Check with your local school system(s) to get the requirements for subbing in the schools in your area. More than likely, you will need some college credit hours and will be subject to a background check.

Temporary Agencies

Working a temporary job can be a good way to get out into the business community, keep your mind active, and potentially learn new skills through computer classes that some agencies offer their clients. Temp work can be a good step towards a permanent position in areas such as general clerical, medical, customer service, and manual labor especially. Employers like the option of trying out an employee before buying, so to speak.

In my experience, temp agencies, unless specialized (ex. healthcare) or focused on contracted assignments (ex. IT), are not the greatest places to find long-term professional level positions. The honest reality is that in the smaller towns and cities, you are less likely to find these specialized firms.

My advice when temping is to check in often with your firm, emphasize your desire to work, and always present yourself professionally. Some bigger staffing services companies include

Adecco
http://www.adeccousa.com/

Express Personnel Services
http://www.expresspersonnel.com/

Kelly Services
http://www.kellyservices.com

Labor Ready
http://www.laborready.com/

Manpower
http://www.manpower.com

OfficeTeam
http://www.officeteam.com/

Randstad
http://www.randstad.com

Snelling
http://www.snelling.com

Healthcare
Interim HealthCare
http://www.interimhealthcare.com/

NurseFinders
http://www.nursefinders.com

Also, check out temporary staffing companies that are locally or regionally owned. They often have numerous contacts within the community.

Major points to keep in mind with all short term employment opportunities are

- Always be on time and dress appropriately for the job. Ask the employer up front about the dress code. Ask the placement coordinator at the temporary agency or human resources person what is expected. Numerous times, I have seen people report for a short term job dressed like they just rolled out of bed or are headed out to solicit (if you know what I mean) when the regular work day is over.

- Give the employer your full attention while he or she is explaining your job duties. Take notes if needed, make sure that your cell phone is turned off, and ask any questions that you need to, to clarify your job responsibilities.

- Be kind and polite to everyone that you meet at your job assignment. Not everyone may be kind to you at first (fear that you might take his or her job, you are a stranger, etc. . .). If you show an ability to get along with lots of different employees at a business, the boss will be impressed.

Long Term Option to Consider

One option that you may want to consider if you are driven, organized, detail-oriented, and would enjoy working for yourself, is to start a business. This decision is not for the faint of heart and would certainly be more involved, more difficult, and more risky than working for someone else much of the time. You should thoroughly explore what is involved in starting a business before you ever step in that direction. Owning your own business can rewarding if done right.

CHAPTER FOUR

Quick Tips From Experience:
I Have Lived Through the Pain,
So You Can Avoid It.

Having been on both the interviewee and interviewer sides of the desk many times, I have had my share of job searching adventures. Below are some tips that I hope will propel you along in your search while keeping you out of the potholes.

Resumes That Make a Statement

- Neutral color and nice paper stock is the general rule unless applying for a job in a field such as creative services where the employer is receptive to alternatives. Skip the white copier paper you borrowed from your neighbor.

- Make SURE that no words are misspelled on your resume and that you keep your information concise. One tip for catching mistakes is to have three other people read over your resume for spelling and grammatical errors. If you do not have three friends that you can arm twist to do some proofing, read your resume backwards to look for mistakes.

- For goodness sake, do not use white-out on a resume. I received a resume in the mail one time that looked like it had crusty mounds of snow all over it. I didn't want to touch it, much less read it.

- Stick to Arial, Times New Roman, or other readable fonts. Do not get fancy.

- No birth dates, hobbies, weight, height, pet's or children's names should be listed or photographs attached to the resume unless specifically requested. DO include a phone number where you can easily be reached.

- Send your resume to a specific person or persons whenever possible. Check spellings of names before you send the resume out.

- Make sure that the stamp that you use on your letter is professional looking. In other words, if they just came out with the tribute to wrestling stamps, please do not use the Hulk the Bulk stamp smacked across the front of your envelope.

- Develop hardcopy and e-mail ready versions of your resume so that you will be prepared for all situations. The Internet has lots of great references on how to develop these formats.

- Distribute your resume to carefully selected businesses. I personally do not recommend using an online resume distributor or resume blaster. These services send hundreds of copies of your resume out to businesses or contacts on their lists. I personally think that by using these services and distributing your resumes for thousands of people online to access, you are putting yourself at risk for misuse of your personal information. Just my opinion.

Cover Letters That Command Attention

- Hold your cover letter to one page, always address it to a specific person(s), and print it on the same paper that you use for your resume.

- If applying for an advertised job, be sure and incorporate keywords from the job description throughout your cover letter. I often take out my highlighter pen and mark off those words from the ad as I put them in the cover letter to keep track.

- For networking and general job inquiry cover letters, highlight your experience using words and phrases that indicate skills that are prized in your field of interest. To come up with these words and phrases, check out professional association websites for your field, the websites of businesses who specialize in your line of work and job ads from other parts of the country for the position(s) that you are looking for.

- Never staple your cover letter to your resume unless specifically requested to do so.

Portfolios and Putting Them Together

One item that can give you an edge over the competition faster than anything else that I have ever seen is a well put together portfolio of your work.

- Gather between ten and twelve samples of your work if possible (research papers, work projects, sample pieces from community or club involvement, etc…)

- Go to an art store or browse online at an art or photography supply site for a portfolio display case. These cases come in a variety of shapes and sizes and some even look much like a briefcase (which is great).

- For work samples that interviewers can view without flipping pages such as a one page flyer or photograph, spray mount those to your display pages. This mounting keeps your items from sliding around and falling out of your display case when you open it. Spray mount is readily available at craft and art supply stores. For reports and other multi-page items, stick them in a side pocket of the display case.

- If applicable, put together a version of your portfolio on CD or DVD or as a website so that interviewers can view at their leisure. See the additional resources section of this book for information on developing this type of portfolio.

- Bring your portfolio to all interviews, but always wait for the interviewer to request to see it before you display it. I have gone on a number of interviews where I was never requested to show the portfolio, but the fact that I had one really worked in my favor.

A Word on Phone Etiquette and Answering Machines

- Record a professional outgoing answering machine message so that employers' first impression of you will be positive when you are not available to answer the phone yourself. In the message, you should make sure that you list the phone number called and specify that you will return the call as soon as possible.

- When participating in a phone interview, make sure that you are in a quiet room with no distractions. Take notes on information that the company interviewer gives you and make sure that you have questions prepared for the interviewer should you be asked.

- Never chew gum, smoke, eat, drink, or watch TV during a phone interview. The phone enhances sounds and the interviewer will pick up on what is going on.

Impressive Dress

- No matter the size of the business or town, dress as if you are interviewing for the big boss's job. Overdressing wins out over underdressing any day. Nicely pressed and freshly laundered clothes are a must.

- Avoid perfume, tobacco smoke smells, clunky jewelry, cartoon character ties, bubble gum, bright red nail polish, sandals, makeup as thick as the powder on a ski slope, and prolific dandruff. (I have seen, smelled, or heard them all).

- Guys, make sure your socks match your suit. I had a guy come in one time for a job interview wearing a black suit with bright red knee socks. Let's just say that was the high point of his interview.

- Women, if giving a standing presentation in front of a group as part of the interview, I recommend flats. I learned from a not so fun experience, that leg shakes are often uncontrollable in high heels. Also for the women, carry along an extra pair of panty hose, some nail polish for hose runs, and some spot wipes in your purse.

- Everybody, pop a breath mint before you enter the business. It helps ensure fresh breath and combats the dreaded dry mouth.

Operation Lobby Reconnaissance

Your wait in the lobby before your interview is invaluable time for company research.

- First and foremost, check out the employees that wander through the lobby as you are waiting. In general, do they look happy, sad, mad, etc. . . ? What kind of things do you overhear employees talking about (all the while acting like you are not listening to their conversation at all)? I will give you a personal example. I heard a guy at an Internet startup where I was interviewing tell a co-worker that he had so much work that he had not been home in 48 hours nor had he slept during that time. RED FLAG! RED FLAG! If you work here, you will not have a life!

- Check out the walls. Do you see employee satisfaction awards, newspaper articles about company accolades, individual employee awards, etc. . . ? What condition is the lobby in? Shabby surrounding may mean that the place is operating on a shoestring budget.

Face-to-Face

The face-to-face interview is your real chance to shine. You will be evaluated from the minute you set foot into the building until you depart. Be nice to everyone you meet along the way. You never know who the boss will ask to give their opinions about you.

- Do your research before you come to interview and try your best to be yourself during the interview. If it is any consolation, most of the people on the other side of the table dislike conducting interviews, as much as, you dislike having to go through them.

- There are many more amateur interviewers than there are professionals. You may notice things like an interviewer reading your resume for the first time as he or she sits down to talk to you or that phone calls and visits keep interrupting the interviewer. The interviewer may even seem unsure of what to ask. See these things as signs that you have a multi-tasking worker interviewing you and let that put you at ease. Take initiative and tell this person how much you could assist him or her by lightening his or her workload.

- If you happen to be interviewed by a panel of people, remember that many of them may have been asked to interview you minutes before. Do not be unnerved by someone rereading your resume in your presence, or by the one person on the panel who thinks it would be great to try out all the humdinger interview questions that he or she can think of. Speak to the group as a whole periodically making eye contact with each person in the room. At the end of the interview, thank everyone in the room for their time and reiterate your desire for the job.

Questions, Questions, So Many Questions

Ah! The dreaded "what will they ask me" anxiety. So many possibilities, so many answers. Let me help you out here. Over time I have noticed through experience that certain questions pop up over and over again.

- *So How Long Have You Lived Here?* (If your answer indicates quite a while, this question will be followed with) *What school did you go to? Where do you live? Do you have family who live here? What are their names?* If you answer that you have recently moved to the area, you will get questions such as *What made you move here? Do you like it here? Are you planning to stay here for a while?* (In smaller town terms, you are an "outsider" and the interviewer is sizing you up to see if you have potential to become a "long timer").

- *So what would you like to tell me about yourself?* This question is not a green light to launch into "my favorite hobby is competitive belching and I have dog named Stud." Instead put your research about the company and the traits needed for the job into play. For example, you can start your answer with, "I am detail oriented, work well in individual and group settings, and can multi-task, etc. . .

- *What are your greatest strengths?* Reiterate traits that relate directly to the job at hand.

- *What is your greatest weakness?* Tread carefully here. The interviewer would like for you to reveal reasons that he or she should rule you out for a job. The best answer to this question turns a negative into a positive. For example, "I do not like filing, but I have learned to do a good job at it by making a game out of it."

- *What accomplishment are you most proud of?* This question gives you an opportunity to show how you have excelled, but at the same time indicate that you have saved your best work for the job for which you are interviewing. For example, as part of a team, you helped developed a product improvement that saved your company thousands of dollars. In the process, you learned how you can save even more money the next time.

- *What has been your most challenging work situation so far?* You might want to list a work project that you learned a lot from and explain how you grew from the experience.

- *How do you handle someone who is angry with you?* This question is designed to reveal how you handle conflict. Are you a hothead, a diffuser, or somewhere in between? The cooler a cucumber you are in the heat of battle, the better.

- *Where do you see yourself in five years?* I think this is my least favorite question. The best answer should illustrate how you will continue making solid and essential contributions to the company.

- *What would your friends or past employers say about you?* Once again reiterate your strengths.

- *What kind of salary are you expecting for this job?* Never blurt out a figure when you are asked. Your first comment should be to ask the interviewer what range the company is looking to pay for this position. If the interviewer will not answer, then you can offer a range with your desired salary in the middle.

- *Why should I hire you over the other seven candidates I am interviewing?* Emphasize your skills and what you can bring to the workplace. Never talk badly about other people. Simply highlight your unique strengths and background.

The "Did You Have to Go There" Questions

Unfortunately, I have had to deal with my share of "illegal" questions. Many interviewers know that what they are asking is not appropriate, but figure why not ask anyway. A few ask out of ignorance of the law, but not many. And face it folks, many employers figure that most people will not spend the time and money to try to publicly call them on the carpet over these questions.

- Some "illegal" questions you might be prepared for include: *Are you married? Will you need our daycare services? Do you have children or plan on having children? Do you really think that you will be an effective worker if you become pregnant?*

  The best one I have ever been asked is, "*Why do you want to work; can't your husband support you?*" I was just about ready to get the boxing gloves out on that one.

- When you get asked an inappropriate question, you have several options. You can say that the question is not appropriate and that you will not answer it. The employer will not like this answer and will be likely to rule you out of contention for the job because of it. If you have already determined that the job is not for you, then this response may be a viable option.

If you do want this job, you might say something to the effect of "My personal life will not affect my ability to be a very successful and productive employee." Repeat as many times as necessary throughout the interview.

Also, if the employer asks something that you feel like answering, you can do that too. However, one thing to consider with an interviewer that asks lots of personal questions is whether you want to work with this type of person and company.

Thank Yous Are So Sweet

At the end of the interview, be sure and thank the interviewer for his or her time and repeat your interest in the job. When you get home, be sure to type up a thank you note and drop it in the mail right away. Since so few people remember to write thank you notes anymore, you will stand out.

On page 94, I will offer an example of a resume that illustrates some of the most common mistakes that people make on these job documents. See if you can spot the mistakes.

Here are a few hints to help you. Spelling is a big problem for many people. So is tendency to undersell accomplishments and skills. What about information that has no place on a resume? How about the overall look of a resume? Is that important?

By the way, according to the *Handbook for Proofreading[1]*, some commonly misspelled and confused words include (none of which have been misspelled in the exercise on the opposite page).

a, an

accept, except

capitol, capital

compare to, compare with

ensure, insure

lay, lie

principal, principle

rise, raise

Check the above book out for many more listings.

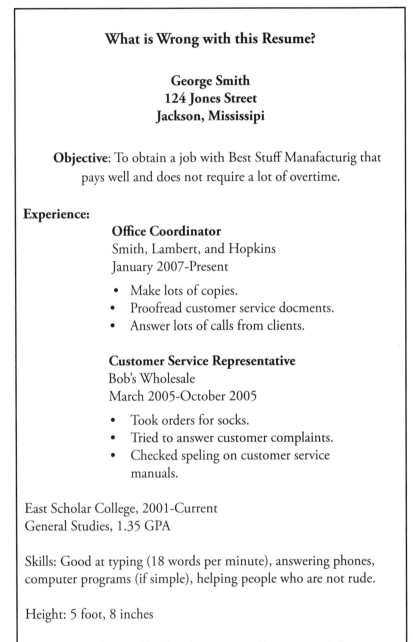

What is Wrong with this Resume?

George Smith
124 Jones Street
Jackson, Mississipi

Objective: To obtain a job with Best Stuff Manafacturig that pays well and does not require a lot of overtime.

Experience:

Office Coordinator
Smith, Lambert, and Hopkins
January 2007-Present

- Make lots of copies.
- Proofread customer service docments.
- Answer lots of calls from clients.

Customer Service Representative
Bob's Wholesale
March 2005-October 2005

- Took orders for socks.
- Tried to answer customer complaints.
- Checked speling on customer service manuals.

East Scholar College, 2001-Current
General Studies, 1.35 GPA

Skills: Good at typing (18 words per minute), answering phones, computer programs (if simple), helping people who are not rude.

Height: 5 foot, 8 inches

Love to waterski, read books, shop,rest, and have pet gerbil named Buzzard.

Explanation of Mistakes in the Resume

George Smith
124 Jones Street
Jackson, Mississipi

(Did you notice that Mississippi is misspelled? How about the lack of a phone number and e-mail address?)

Objective: To obtain a job with Best Stuff Manafacturig that pays well and does not require a lot of overtime.

(Manufacturing is misspelled. Do I want to hire someone who can't spell my company's name? Also, does George really want to mention how he is not willing to work extra time? What a first impression!)

Experience

Office Coordinator
Smith, Lambert, and Hopkins
January 2007-Present

- Make lots of copies.
- Proofread customer services docments.
- Answer lots of calls from clients.

(Misspelled word documents in the same sentence he is talking about proofreading. Hmm.)

Customer Service Representative
Bob's Wholesale
March 2005-October 2006

- Took orders for socks
- Tried to answer customer complaints.
- Checked speling on customer service manuals.

(Did you notice that spelling is misspelled. George has really undersold his skills and experience. He can do so much better on the descriptions while still being concise.)

East Scholar College, 2001-Current
General Studies, 1.35 GPA
(Why emphasize a less than stellar GPA. In this case, George is better off leaving that information off of his resume. Also, he needs to be prepared in an interview to provide an explanation of the length of time he is taking to get a degree and where he is in the process.)

Skills: Good at typing (18 words per minute), answering phones, computer programs (if simple), helping people who are not rude.
(Once again, George underplays his skills and shows his weaknesses. His typing speed and computer programs skill levels do not look good as written. Also, including the comment about helping people who are not rude will make the employer wonder about his true customer service skills, especially his patience.)

Height: 5 foot, 8 inch
(Do not include personal information about height, weight, or a photograph unless specifically asked to do so because of physical requirements for the job.)

Hobbies: Love to waterski, read books, shop, rest and have pet gerbil named Buzzard.
(There is such a thing as too much information. How does having a pet gerbil named Buzzard qualify you for a job?)

In addition to the items that have been mentioned, did you notice that George did not include

- Information about any professional associations that he belongs to.

- List of any civic or community involvements that he may have that would be relevant to the job that he is seeking.

- Mention of the fact that he is ready to provide references upon request.

A More Powerful Resume

George Smith
124 Jones Street
Jackson, Mississippi
Phone: 101-551-1010
E-mail: george@email.net

Objective: To obtain a manufacturing customer support manager position in a challenging and fast-paced environment.

Experience:

Office Coordinator
Smith, Lambert, and Hopkins
January 2007-Present
- Respond to client calls and match clients with service providers.
- Ensure accuracy of customer service documents in order to provide excellent customer care.
- Oversee workflow for a 15 person staff.

Customer Service Representative
Bob's Wholesale
March 2005- October 2006
- Handled 750 customer orders for apparel a month.
- Resolved customer issues and contributed to the company's ninety-nine percent satisfaction rating.

Member: Wholesalers and Manufacturers Support Association

Awards: Customer Service Gold Standard Provider

References Available Upon Request

CHAPTER FIVE

The Resources Roundup: A Little Something Extra

Although, we have looked at a number of great resources to help you on your way to a successful job search, I want to include a listing of some extras in case you want to dive deeper into a particular topic.

Career Exploration Resources

Websites

About.com Jobs and Careers Section

http://about.com/careers/

At this site, check out careers by category, use the salary comparison tool, and even do a quick search for jobs.

Keirsey.com

http://www.keirsey.com

This site contains the Keirsey Temperament Sorter questionnaire and descriptions of the personality temperaments. You will need to register to take the questionnaire.

CareerOne Stop

http://www.careeronestop.org

- In depth exploration of occupations, including state and national employment, and wage trends for those jobs
- Industry reports that include health of the industry
- State specific job resources information

Career and Educational Guidance Center at the University of California at Berkeley

http://www.uhs.berkeley.edu/Students/CareerLibrary/links/career.cfm

At this career center, find details on professions ranging from agriculture to social sciences.

Career Voyages- Career Exploration Site

http://www.careervoyages.gov

This website is the result of collaboration between the U.S. Department of Labor and the U.S. Department of Education. It is designed to provide information on high growth, in-demand occupations, along with details about the skills and education needed to attain those jobs.

JobStar Central's Guide to Specific Careers

http://jobstar.org/tools/career/spec-car.php

Find detailed information about careers ranging from accounting to travel agency work at this site.

Occupational Outlook Handbook
http://www.bls.gov/oco/home.htm
Through this handbook get detailed information on numerous occupations, average salaries in particular regions, and reviews of the health and outlooks for various industries.

O*Net Occupational Information Network
http://online.onetcenter.org/
The O*NET system offers occupational information and provides detailed information on key attributes and characteristics of workers and occupations.

PersonalityType.com
http://www.personalitytype.com/
Interesting information can be found here about personality type discovery and careers that match types.

Books
Bolles, Richard Nelson. *What Color Is Your Parachute? 2008: A Practical Manual for Job-Hunters and Career-Changers.* Berkeley: Ten Speed Press, 2007.

Damp, Dennis V. *The Book of U.S. Government Jobs: Where They Are, What's Available & How to Get One.* 10th Ed. McKees Rocks, PA: Bookhaven Press, 2008.

Damp, Dennis V. *Post Office Jobs: Explore and Find Jobs, Prepare for the 473 Postal Exam, and Locate ALL Job Opportunities.* 4th Ed. McKees Rocks, PA: Bookhaven Press, 2005.

Great Jobs Book Series. New York: McGraw-Hill.

Opportunities In Book Series. New York: McGraw-Hill.

The United States Department of Labor. *Big Book of Jobs 2007-2008.* New York: McGraw-Hill, 2006 and 2007.

The United States Department of Labor. *Occupational Outlook Handbook, 2007-2008 Edition.* St. Paul, MN: JIST Publishing, 2008.

Vault Career Guides from the Vault Career Library
Examples:
Alba, Jason. *Vault Career Guide to Accounting.* 2nd ed. New York: Vault, Inc., 2005.

Kukoff, David *Vault Career Guide to Screenwriting Careers.* New York: Vault, Inc., 2005.

Business and Organization Research Resources
Websites
AnnualReports.com
http://www.annualreports.com/

This website offers a free online look at numerous company annual reports.

AnyWho: Internet Directory Assistance
http://www.anywho.com
This directory offers yellow and white pages lookups as well as reverse telephone lookups.

Inc.Com's Best Cities for Doing Business
http://www.inc.com/bestcities/index.html
Inc.com breaks down its ranking of best cities to do business in by large, midsize, and small cities.

MapQuest
http://www.mapquest.com/
Check out the location of a business and its surroundings, as well as, get driving directions. The company offers a variety of ways to receive mapping information (both wired and wireless).

McGraw Hill Construction
http://www.construction.com/
Check out the company's regional construction directories online to get the names of contacts in the industry.

New York Public Library
http://www.nypl.org/research/sibl/trade/index.cfm
This page shows information links to industry specific directories for numerous fields. This material may help you find out what

directories to be on the look out for based on your specific career interest.

Spoke
http://www.spoke.com/
This website allows you to access a database of over 35 million contacts at companies. You can search down by job title, industry, and geographic location. Many of the services of Spoke are free, but a hefty monthly fee is required to access all features.

ZoomInfo
http://www.zoominfo.com
This resource provides information on millions of businesses and individuals that may be helpful during your research or an interview. In order to obtain executive level profiles, you will need to pay a good size monthly fee.

Below are examples of agencies and offices that can be found in most, if not all states, to allow you to further explore government jobs. Agencies may go by various names depending on the states, but perform many of the same functions. The following listings offer links to these state sites, as well as, some examples of the types of jobs available statewide and many times regionally with these organizations.

State Agricultural Departments
State and Local Government on the Net
http://www.statelocalgov.net/50states-agriculture.cfm

(Agricultural Commodity Grader, Agricultural Inspector, Forester, Hydrologist, Mosquito Control Technician)

State Corrections Departments
The911Site.com
 http://www.the911site.com/911pd/us_corrections.shtml#state
(Chaplains, Correctional Officers, Plumbers, Social Workers, Teachers)

State Courts
National Center for State Courts
http://www.ncsconline.org/D_KIS/info_court_web_sites
html#State
(Communications Systems Operator, Custody Evaluator Deputy Clerk, Probation Officer, Social Worker (Criminal Justice))

State Emergency Management Agencies
FEMA
http://www.fema.gov/about/contact/statedr.shtm
(Disaster Preparedness Program Director, Emergency Management Watch Officer, Mitigation Planning Coordinator, Security Guard, Training and Education Coordinator)

State Fish and Wildlife Agencies
U.S. Fish & Wildlife Service
http://www.fws.gov/offices/statelinks.html
(Accountant, Biologist, Game Warden, Software Developer, Water Resources Engineer)

State Health Agencies
U.S. Food and Drug Administration
http://www.fda.gov/oca/sthealth.htm
(Comprehensive Health Planner, Epidemiologist, Registered Nurse, Speech Pathologist, Toxicologist)

State Motor Vehicle Services
USA.gov
http://www.usa.gov/Topics/Motor_Vehicles.shtml
(Customer Representative Associate, Driver's License Examiner, Motor Vehicle Emissions Agent, Motor Vehicle Field Representative, Personnel Officer (Test Development Specialist))

State Purchasing and Procurement Agencies
National Association of State Procurement Officials
http://www.naspo.org/directors/
(Assistant Purchasing Agent, Category Manager, Human Resources Director, Process Improvement Manager, Supply, Storage, and Distribution Technician)

State Tax and Revenue Agencies
Internal Revenue Service
http://www.irs.gov/taxpros/article/0,,id=100236,00.html
(Data Entry Operator, Information Technology Administrator, Revenue Agent, Revenue Field Examiner, Tax Examiner)

State Veterans Affairs Offices
United States Department of Veterans Affairs

http://www.va.gov/statedva.htm
(Claims Examiner, Dental Technologist, Police Officer, Public Affairs Specialist, Utility Systems Repairer)

USA.Gov
http://www.usa.gov/Agencies/State_and_Territories/Agencies_by_Topic.shtml
For a comprehensive list of government offices and agencies check this site out.

Job Hotlines and Websites
You may also want to check out some of the job search telephone hotlines that are often available through businesses, government agencies, and public entities at all levels to see what type of jobs these organizations are offering. You are going to have to search by keywords to get to what you want in regards to these hotlines as I can find no one comprehensive online guide to the hotlines. The hotline craze has faded some as Internet job listings have really taken hold.

If you want to check out an example of the job hotlines resources that you may run into look at

University of Minnesota Morris Career Center
http://www.morris.umn.edu/services/career/job_postings/hotline.php
Job hotline listings on this website range from the CIA to a major hospital center's listings.

Books

Look for State Manufacturers' Directories or Registers for your particular state at your local library, generally in the reference section.

Cubbage, Sue and Marcia Williams. *National Job Hotline Directory: The Job Finder's Hot List.* River Forest, IL: Planning Communications, 1999.

Gottlieb, Richard. *Directory of Business Information Resources.* Millerton, NY: Grey House Publishing, 2007.

Lynch, Margaret. *Hoover's MasterList of U.S. Companies.* 14th Ed. Austin, TX: Hoover's Business Press, 2008.

Romaniuk, Bohdan. *National Directory of Nonprofit Organizations.* 20th Ed. Farmington Hills, MI: Taft Group, 2007.

General Job Search Resources

Books

Dikel, Margaret Riley and Frances E. Roehm. *Guide to Internet Job Searching 2008-2009 Edition.* New York: McGraw-Hill, 2008.

Lauber, Daniel and Deborah Verlench. *Nonprofits Job Finder: Where the Jobs are in Charities & Nonprofits.* 5th Ed. River Forest, IL: Planning Communications, 2008.

Yate, Martin. *Knock 'em Dead 2008: The Ultimate Job Search Guide.* Avon, MA: Adams Media, 2007.

Yeung, Rob. *Job-Hunting and Career Change All-In-One For Dummies.* Hoboken, NJ: John Wiley and Sons, Ltd., 2007.

Specific Job Search Situation Resources
Books

Kissane, Sharon F. *Career Success for People with Physical Disabilities.* Lincolnwood, IL: Vgm Career Horizons, 1997.

Rich, Jason. *202 High Paying Jobs You Can Land Without a College Degree.* Irvine, CA; Entrepreneur Press, 2006.

Woodward, Jeannette. *Finding a Job After 50: Reinvent Yourself for the 21st Century.* Franklin Lakes, NJ: Career Press, 2007.

Networking Resources
Websites

About.com: Job Searching
http://jobsearch.about.com/od/networking/Job_Search
Networking.htm
This section of About.com's site focuses on links to networking articles and sample networking letters and thank you notes.

CareerJournal.com –Networking Section
http://www.careerjournal.com/jobhunting/networking/
Check out a variety of articles on lots of aspects of networking.

Books

Boothman, Nicholas. *How to Connect in Business in 90 Seconds or Less.* New York: Workman Publishing Company, 2002.

Carnegie, Dale. *How to Win Friends & Influence People.* New York: Pocket Books, 1998.

RoAne, Susan. *How to Work a Room: Your Essential Guide to Savvy Socializing.* New York: HarperCollins, 2007.

Spelling and Grammar Resources

Websites

grammar-monster.com
http://www.grammar-monster.com/
Polish your English grammar skills with lessons on punctuation, parts of speech, and illustrations of common language usage errors.

Merriam-Webster Online
http://www.merriam-webster.com/
Quick word/definition lookups and use of a thesaurus to get alternative word suggestions are available at this site. To get access to the unabridged or collegiate versions of the dictionary, you must pay a premium monthly or yearly fee. I recommend keeping a good hard-copy dictionary on hand along with this reference.

The Owl at Purdue
Workplace Writers Section
http://owl.english.purdue.edu/owl/resource/681/01/
Skills checklists for resumes and cover letters, action verb lists, and great writing resources can be found at this site.

Books
Merriam-Webster's Dictionary and Thesaurus. Springfield, MA: Merriam-Webster, 2007.

Shertzer, Margaret. *The Elements of Grammar.* New York: Longman, 1996.

Straus, Jane. *The Blue Book of Grammar and Punctuation: An Easy-to-Use Guide to Clear Rules, Real-World Examples, and Reproducible Quizzes.* 10th ed. Indianapolis, IN: Jossey-Bass, 2007.

Strunk, William. *The Elements of Style.* Claremont: CA: Coyote Canyon Press, 2007.

Resume, Cover Letter, Interviewing, and Portfolio Resources

Websites
CAREERMagic
http://www.career-magic.com/index.resources.html
This site offers good articles on the subjects of resumes, interviewing, interview attire, and much more.

JobStar Central

http://www.jobstar.org/index.php

This all-purpose job resource site focuses on resume advice, career guides, salary information, networking, etc. . .

Monster.com

http://www.monster.com

The Career Advice section offers:

- Interview Center (all about interviews)
- Job profiles
- Resume Center with articles and activities
- Salary Center with information about pay, negotiating, benefits, etc. . .
- Self-Assessment Center with a variety of tests to determine more about yourself and your interests
- Advice about specific situations such as career change, contract and temporary work, and military and veterans' employment
- Miscellaneous other resources

Purdue University's Online Writing Lab Workshop for Cover Letters

http://owl.english.purdue.edu/owl/resource/681/01/

This hypertext workshop found in this section walks you through the steps to put together an effective cover letter.

WorkBloom

http://workbloom.com/default.aspx

WorkBloom contains resume, cover letter, and interview advice; as well as, a daily employment news blog.

Yahoo! Hotjobs

http://hotjobs.yahoo.com/careertools

Career Tools section offers resources related to:

- Articles on job search, resume prep, interviewing, and networking
- Salary calculator and benefits information
- Job board to communicate with other job seekers
- Newsletter sign-ups
- Personality and career assessment tests and other resources

Portfolio Specific Websites

About.com

http://jobsearch.about.com/cs/resumes/a/portfolio.htm

This section of the site focuses largely on the creation of online portfolios.

QuintCareers.com

http://quintcareers.4jobs.com/MKT/Content/JS/Default.asp?pg=Portfolio

Section focuses on building a complete career portfolio.

Books

Cover Letters

Yate, Martin. *Cover Letters That Knock'em Dead.* 7th ed. Avon, MA: Adams Media, 2006.

Interviews

DeLuca, Matthew J. *Best Answers to the 201 Most Frequently Asked Interview Questions.* New York: McGraw-Hill, 1996.

Kador, John. *201 Best Questions to Ask On Your Interview.* New York: McGraw-Hill, 2002.

Oliver, Vicky. *301 Smart Answers to Tough Interview Questions.* Naperville, IL: Sourcebooks, 2005.

Wallace, Richard. *Adams Job Interview Almanac.* 2nd ed. Avon, MA: Adams Media, 2005

Portfolios

Satterthwaite, Frank, and Gary D'Orsi. *The Career Portfolio Workbook: Using the Newest Tool in Your Job-Hunting Arsenal to Impress Employers and Land a Great Job!* New York: McGraw-Hill, 2002.

Resumes

Block, Jay A., and Michael Betrus. *101 Best Resumes.* New York: McGraw-Hill, 1997.

Kennedy, Joyce Lain. *Resumes for Dummies.* 5th ed. Hoboken, NJ: Wiley Publishing, 2007.

Krannich, Ron. *Resume, Application and Letter Tips for People with Hot and Not-So-Hot Backgrounds: 185 Tips for Landing the Perfect Job.* Manassas Park, VA: Impact Publications, 2006.

McKinney, Anne is the author for all of the following:

Real-Resumes for Administrative Support, Office & Secretarial Jobs. Fayetteville, NC: PREP Publishing, 2004.

Real-Resumes for Aviation and Travel Jobs: Including Real Resumes Used to Change Careers and Transfer Skills to Other Industries. Fayetteville, NC: PREP Publishing, 2002.

Real-Resumes for Auto Industry Jobs: Including Real Resumes Used to Change Careers and Resumes Used to Gain Federal Employment. Fayetteville, NC: PREP Publishing, 2003.

Real-Resumes for Computer Jobs. Fayetteville, NC: PREP Publishing, 2001.

Real-Resumes for Construction Jobs: Including Real Resumes Used to Change Careers and Transfer Skills to Other Industries. Fayetteville, NC: PREP Publishing, 2002.

Real-Resumes for Customer Service Jobs: Including Real Resumes Used to Change Careers and Resumes Used to Gain Federal Employment. Fayetteville, NC: PREP Publishing, 2005.

Real-Resumes for Engineering Jobs. Fayetteville, NC: PREP Publishing, 2004.

Real-Resumes for Financial Jobs. Fayetteville, NC: PREP Publishing, 2001.

Real-Resumes for Firefighting Jobs: Including Real Resumes Used to Change Careers and Gain Federal Employment. Fayetteville, NC: PREP Publishing, 2004.

Real-Resumes for Human Resources and Personnel Jobs: Real Resumes Used to Change Careers and Transfer Skills to Other Industries. Fayetteville, NC: PREP Publishing, 2002.

Real-Resumes for Legal and Paralegal Jobs. Fayetteville, NC: PREP Publishing, 2004.

Real-Resumes for Media, Newspaper, Broadcasting and Public Affairs Jobs: Including Real Resumes Used to Change Careers and Transfer Skills to Other Industries. Fayetteville, NC: PREP Publishing, 2002.

Real-Resumes for Medical Jobs. Fayetteville, NC: PREP Publishing, 2001.

Real-Resumes for Manufacturing Jobs: Including Real Resumes Used to Change Careers and Transfer Skills to Other Industries. Fayetteville, NC: PREP Publishing, 2002.

Real-Resumes for Jobs in Nonprofit Organizations: Including Real Resumes Used to Change Careers and Gain Federal Employment. Fayetteville, NC: PREP Publishing, 2004.

Real-Resumes for Nursing Jobs: Including Real Resumes Used to Change Careers and Resumes Used to Gain Federal Employment. Fayetteville, NC: PREP Publishing, 2003.

Real-Resumes for Police, Law Enforcement and Security Jobs: Including Real Resumes Used to Change Careers and Transfer Skills to Other Industries. Fayetteville, NC: PREP Publishing, 2002.

Real-Resumes for Real Estate & Property Management Jobs. Fayetteville, NC: PREP Publishing, 2006.

Real-Resumes for Restaurant, Food Service and Hotel Jobs: Including Real Resumes Used to Change Careers and Transfer Skills to Other Industries. Fayetteville, NC: PREP Publishing, 2002.

Real-Resumes for Retailing, Modeling, Fashion and Beauty Industry Jobs: Including Real Resumes Used to Change Careers and Transfer Skills to Other Industries. Fayetteville, NC: PREP Publishing, 2002.

Real-Resumes for Safety & Quality Assurance Jobs. Fayetteville, NC: PREP Publishing, 2005.

Real-Resumes for Sales. Fayetteville, NC: PREP Publishing, 2000.

Real-Resumes for Social Work and Counseling Jobs: Including Real Resumes Used to Change Careers and Transfer Skills to Other Industries. Fayetteville, NC: PREP Publishing, 2002.

Real-Resumes for Sports Industry Jobs: Including Real Resumes Used to Change Careers and Transfer Skills to Other Industries. Fayetteville, NC: PREP Publishing, 2004.

Real-Resumes for Students. Fayetteville, NC: PREP Publishing, 2000.

Real-Resumes for Supply & Logistics Jobs. Fayetteville, NC: PREP Publishing, 2006.

Real-Resumes for Teachers Fayetteville, NC: PREP Publishing, 2000.

Real-Resumes for U.S. Postal Service Jobs Fayetteville, NC: PREP Publishing, 2004.

Real Resumix and & Other Resumes for Federal Government Jobs: Including Samples of Real Resumes Used to Apply for Federal Government Jobs. Fayetteville, NC: PREP Publishing, 2003.

Parker, Yana. *Resume Pro: The Professional Guide.* Berkeley, CA: Ten Speed Press, 1993.

Yate, Martin. *Resumes That Knock 'em Dead.* 7th ed. Avon: Adams Media, 2006.

Business Startup Resources

Websites

Score

http://www.score.org/

The website of this organization known for its large group of volunteer business counselors, provides some valuable resources related to starting and running a business. You may want to consider talking to one of these volunteers about your proposed business plans before preceding any further.

U.S. Small Business Administration

http://www.sba.gov/

This site offers you a whole range of resources to help you decide if owning a business is for you. I would recommend that anyone considering that option, check out this site first.

Books

Covello, Joseph and Brian Hazelgren. *Your First Business Plan.* 5th ed. Naperville, IL: Sourcebooks, Inc., 2005.

Harper, Steven C. *The McGraw-Hill Guide to Starting Your Own Business: A Step-by-Step Blueprint for the First Time Entrepreneur.* New York: McGraw-Hill, 2003.

Monosoff, Tamara. *The Mom Inventors Handbook: How to Turn Your Idea Into the Next Big Thing.* New York: McGraw-Hill, 2005.

Norman, Jan. *What No One Ever Tells You About Starting Your Own Business: Real-Life Start-Up Advice from 101 Entrepreneurs.* Chicago: Dearborn Trade Publishing, 2004.

Turner, Marcia Layton. *Unofficial Guide to Starting a Small Business.* 2nd Edition. Hoboken, NJ: John Wiley & Sons, Inc., 2004.

ENDNOTES

Introduction

1. Bureau of Transportation Statistics, "Omnibus Survey", 2003, http://www.bts.gov/press_releases/2003/bts020_03/html/bts020_03.html (accessed July 11, 2007)

2. U.S. Census Bureau, "American Community Survey", 2005, http://www.census.gov/acs/www/ (accessed July 11, 2007)

3. American Lung Association, "State of the Air: 2007 Report", http://lungaction.org/reports/stateoftheair2007.html (accessed June 5, 2007)

4. Bureau of Justice Statistics, "Homicide Trends in the U.S.", 2006 Last Updated, http://www.ojp.usdoj.gov/bjs/homicide/city.htm (accessed June 5, 2007)

Chapter 3

1. Netcraft, "July 2007 Web Server Survey", http://news.netcraft.com (accessed July 10, 2007).

2.Technorati, "About Us", http://technorati.com/about/ (accessed July 10, 2007).

Chapter 4

1. Anderson, Laura Killen. *Handbook for Proofreading*. New York: McGraw-Hill, 1991.

INDEX

ABOUT THE AUTHOR

Sarah Fuller holds a M.A. in Communications and has spent many years in the workplace at both nonprofit and for profit organizations. She also has a significant amount of experience as both an interviewer and interviewee in the medium to small-sized markets about which she writes. Ms. Fuller is the owner of Inquiza Communications,. L.L.C , a company focused on publishing and consulting on job search-related issues. She is a longtime member of the Public Relations Society of America.

With the ever increasing number of information resources available to job seekers, Ms. Fuller saw a need for a book that focused on detailing the search tools and strategies that will work best for non big city searchers. She saw a lack of publications that focused on this segment of job seekers specifically, even though so many people find themselves in this category.

Be sure and check out the Inquiza Communication's website at http://www.inquiza.com for the very latest in job search information. Also, if you would like to share your success story or have suggestions for information that you would like to see in future editions of this book, please send an e-mail to fuller@inquiza.com.